PSYCHIATRY

for kids

Dear Keoni and Connor,

Never stop learning! You can accomplish anything you set your minds to :)

Love,
Dr. Betty & Dr. Braden

First paperback edition November 2023

Book design by Betty Nguyen & Brandon Pham

ISBN 978-1-957557-18-2 (paperback)
ISBN 978-1-957557-95-3 (hardcover)

Published by Black Phoenix Press

www.mdforkids.org

Dedications

Thank you to the friends and family who have supported and loved us unconditionally, and to the mentors who have guided and taught us more than we could have imagined.

Betty & Brandon

Thank you to my parents, who taught me to believe in myself, to my sister who sees the vision, to my wife who supports me on the good days and bad, and to my nieces, whom I hope this book helps the most.

Jake

Psychiatry

(sai-KAI-uh-tree)

the branch of medicine concerned with the study and treatment of mental illness

Mental illnesses are a wide range of conditions related to differences in the brain that affect our thoughts, mood, and behavior.

Unfortunately, some people have negative attitudes and beliefs toward people with mental illnesses. This is called **stigma**.

Because of this stigma, mental illnesses are less commonly discussed, diagnosed, and treated than physical illnesses.

It's normal to feel anxious or worry about things, but **anxiety disorders** cause too much fear or worry that interferes with daily life.

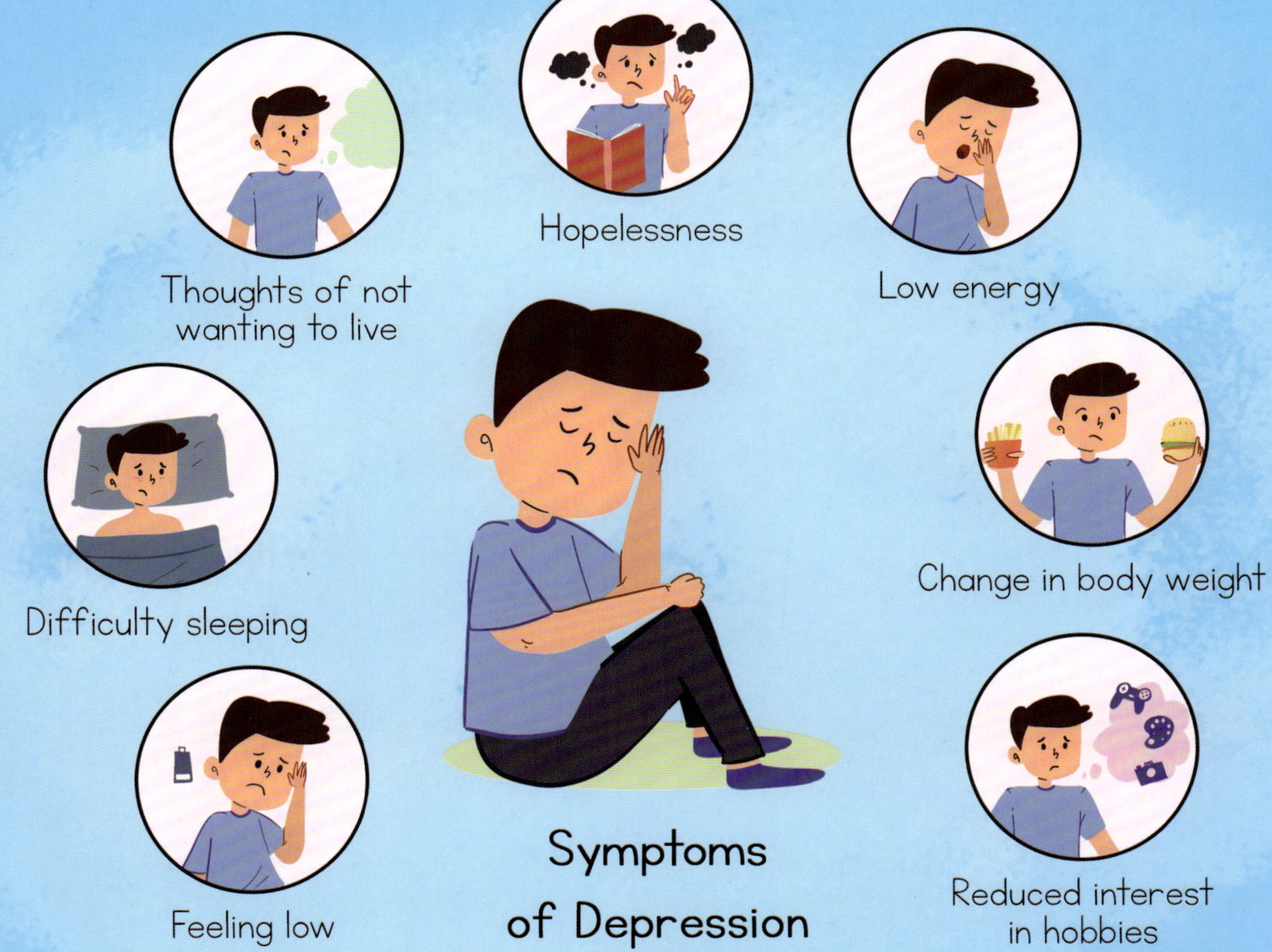

It's also normal to sometimes feel sad, but with **depression**, a sad mood interferes with daily life and can last for weeks, months, or even longer.

Anxiety disorders and depression can be treated with **cognitive behavioral therapy**, which involves meeting with a therapist to talk, learn, and practice skills together.

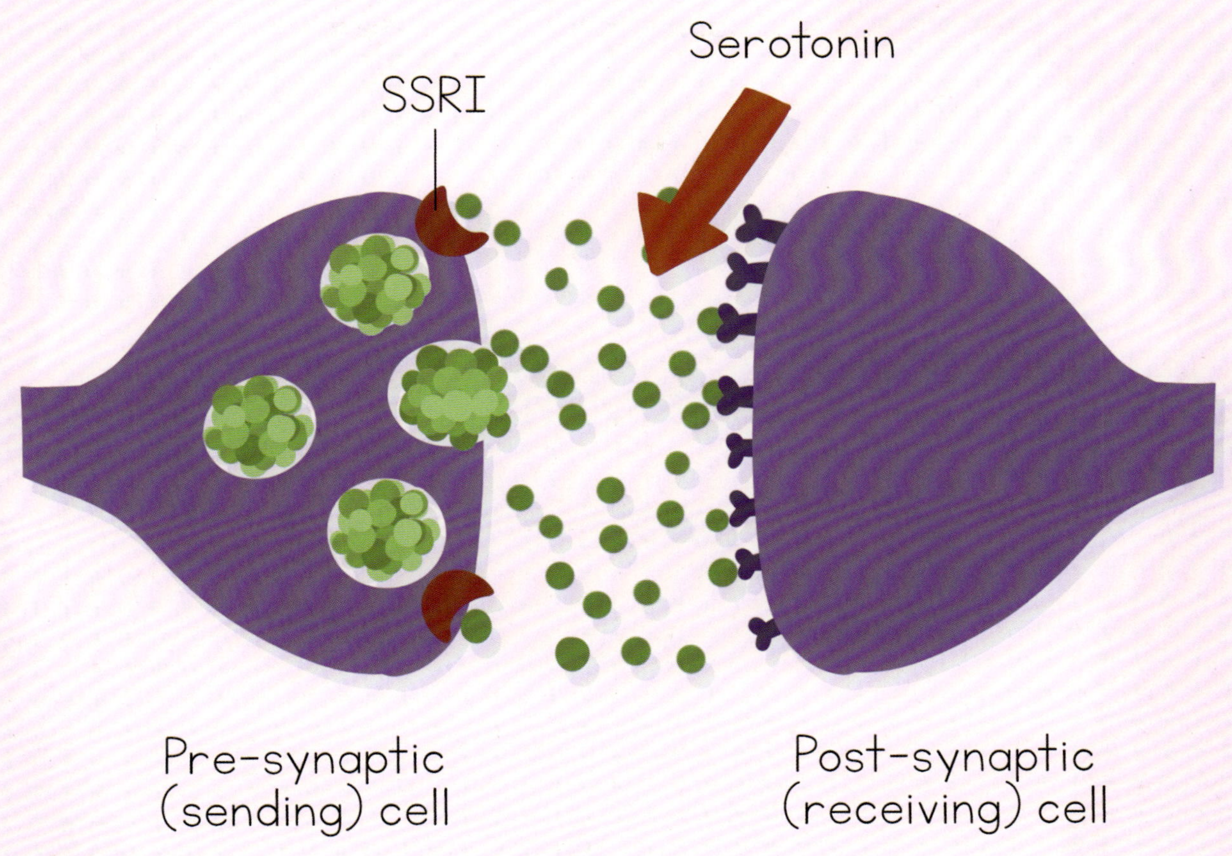

Anxiety disorders and depression can also be treated with medications, such as **selective serotonin reuptake inhibitors (SSRIs)**.

Symptoms of Depressive Episodes

Sadness or hopelessness

Change in appetite

Thoughts of not wanting to live

Fatigue

Difficulty concentrating

Symptoms of Manic Episodes

Excitement or happiness

Fast speech

Distractibility

Overconfidence

Risky behavior

It's normal to have changes in mood, but **bipolar disorder** can cause extreme episodes of sadness (depression) and excitement (mania) that can last for days to weeks.

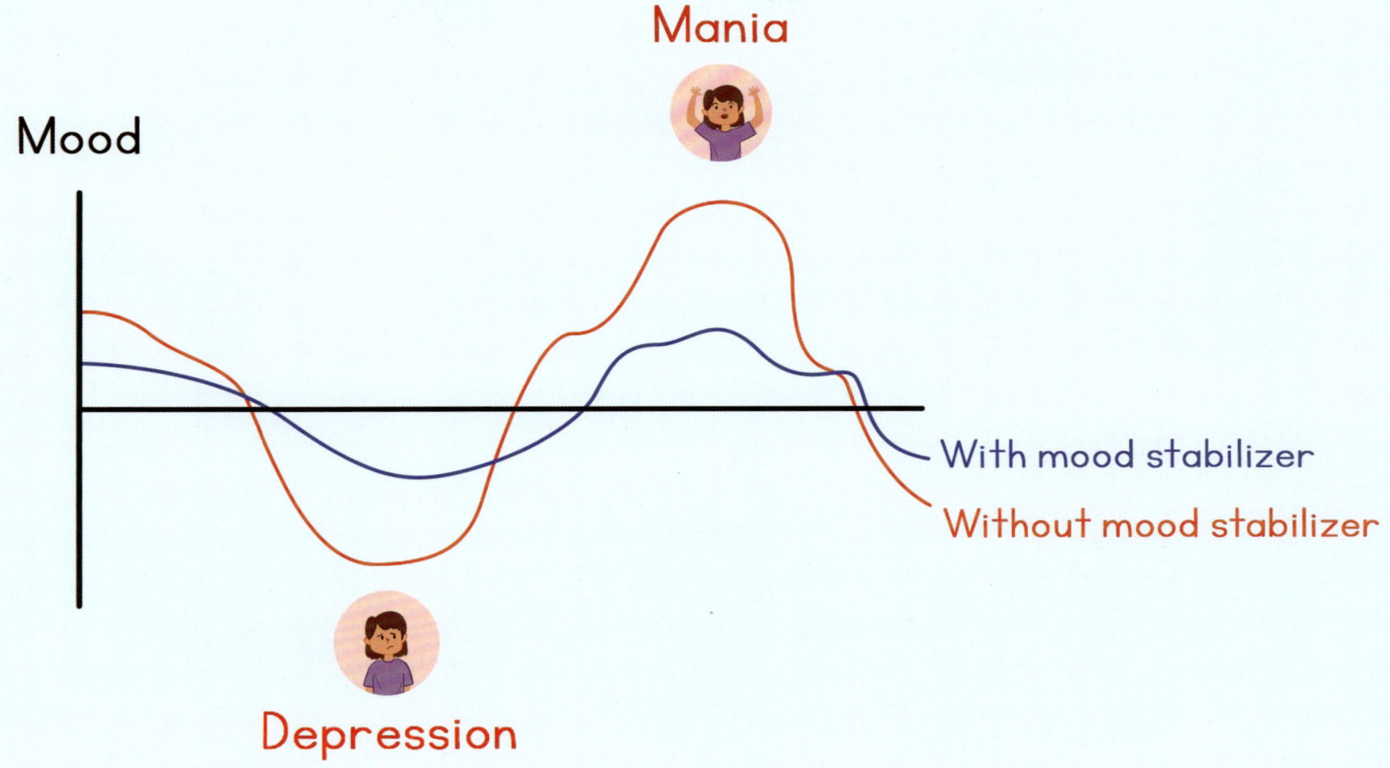

Bipolar disorder can be treated with medications, called **mood stabilzers**, and therapy.

Forgetfulness Carelessness Risky behavior

Symptoms of ADHD

Trouble sitting still Trouble getting along

Daydreaming Excessive talking Disorganization

It's normal to sometimes have trouble paying attention or sitting still, but people with **attention deficit/hyperactivity disorder (ADHD)** struggle with this almost all the time.

ADHD can be treated with medications and therapy. Eating healthy foods and getting enough sleep and exercise can also help!

Obsessive compulsive disorder (OCD) causes repetitive thoughts, called ***obsessions***, which can be followed by structured behaviors, called ***compulsions***.

Like many other mental health conditions, OCD can be treated with a combination of medications and therapy.

Tourette syndrome is a movement disorder that often occurs with ADHD and OCD. It causes repetitive, unintentional movements or sounds called **tics**.

There isn't a cure for Tourette syndrome, but medications and interventions, such as behavioral therapy, can help!

People can sometimes feel unhappy with some parts of their body, but **body dysmorphic disorder** can make it hard for people to stop focusing on their appearance, which can lead to unhealthy habits.

Eating disorders, such as **anorexia** and **bulimia**, cause unhealthy thoughts, feelings, and behaviors about food and body appearance.

We all come in different shapes and sizes! Focusing on things we like about our body can help us maintain a healthy **body image**.

Mental illnesses are not anyone's fault. Just like a physical illness, no one should feel ashamed when experiencing a mental illness.

If you ever want to talk to someone about your feelings, tell a parent, teacher, or doctor. There is always someone who can help!

Developmental disabilities are lifelong conditions that appear during childhood that affect how a person grows, learns, and interacts with others.

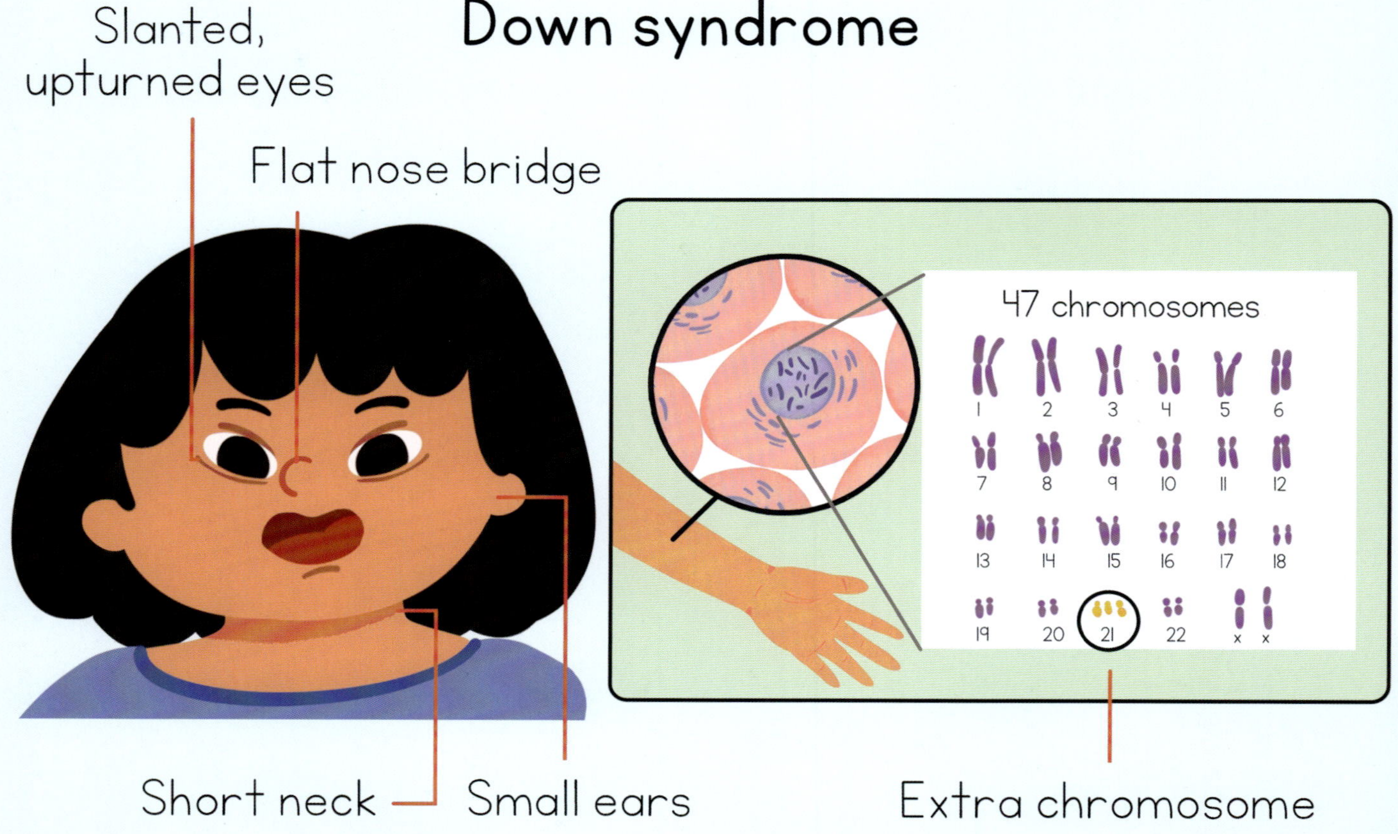

Down syndrome is a developmental disability caused by an error in cell division that leads to an extra copy of a "package" of genes, called a **chromosome**.

Kids with Down syndrome may have trouble learning, but many can attend school, make friends, and work when they're older.

Kids with Down syndrome may need extra help, but they want to be treated the same way as other kids: with love, kindness, and respect.

Autism spectrum disorder, often just called **autism**, is a developmental disability that makes interacting with others more difficult.

People with autism may have different ways of learning, moving, or paying attention. They may also have repetitive behaviors or interests.

Signs of Autism

Repetitive speech or movements

Difficulty communicating

Trouble interpreting how others feel

Prefers to be alone

Avoids eye contact

Eccentric way of moving

Sensitive to loud noises

Recognizing early signs of autism is important because early diagnosis and intervention can improve long-term outcomes.

Genes

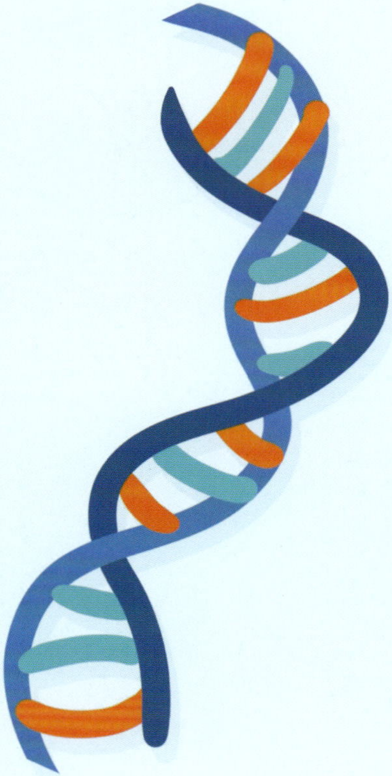

Environment

Most scientists think autism is caused by both genetic and environmental factors. Vaccines do *not* cause autism.

People with developmental disabilities might seem different, but they can live long, healthy, and meaningful lives just like anyone else.

Psychiatrists work on a team alongside therapists, psychologists, and other mental health professionals to treat mental illnesses.

Through therapy and medications, mental health professionals help kids and adults around the world improve their mental health.

YOU'RE A FUTURE PSYCHIATRIST!

Glossary

Anxiety disorders: group of mental illnesses that can cause too much worry, fear, or anxiety that interferes with daily life

Attention deficit/hyperactivity disorder: mental illness that can cause inattention, hyperactivity, and impulsivity

Autism spectrum disorder: developmental disability that makes interacting with others more difficult

Bipolar disorder: mental illness that can cause extreme episodes of sadness (depression) and excitement (mania); can be treated with **mood stabilizers**

Body dysmorphic disorder: mental illness that can cause unhealthy feelings about perceived flaws or defects in appearance

Cognitive behavioral therapy: type of treatment for mental illnesses that involves meeting with a therapist to talk, learn, and practice skills together

Depression: mental illness that can cause persistent feelings of sadness that interferes with daily life

Down syndrome: developmental disability caused by an error in cell division that leads to an extra copy of a "package" of genes, called a chromosome

Eating disorders: mental illnesses, such as anorexia and bulimia, that can cause unhealthy thoughts, feelings, and behaviors about food and body image

Obsessive compulsive disorder: mental illness that causes repetitive thoughts (**obsessions**) that can be followed by structured behaviors (**compulsions**)

Tourette syndrome: movement disorder that causes repetitive, unintentional movements or sounds called **tics**

Let's review what you learned!

1. What group of mental illnesses can cause too much fear or worry that interferes with daily life?
2. What mental illness can cause a sad mood that interferes with daily life?
3. What type of treatment for mental illnesses involves meeting with a therapist to talk, learn, and practice skills together?
4. What class of medications can treat anxiety disorders and depression?
5. What mental illness can cause extreme episodes of sadness (depression) and excitement (mania)? What class of medications can treat this?
6. What mental illness can cause difficulty with paying attention or sitting still? What class of medications can treat this?
7. What mental illness can cause repetitive thoughts, called obsessions, that can be followed by structured behaviors, called compulsions?
8. What movement disorder can cause repetitive, unintentional movements or sounds called tics?
9. What mental illness can cause unhealthy feelings about perceived flaws or defects in appearance?
10. What group of mental illnesses can cause unhealthy thoughts, feelings, and behaviors about food and body image?
11. What developmental disability is caused by an error in cell division that leads to an extra copy of chromosome 21?
12. What developmental disability can make interacting with others difficult?

Your Answers

1. ______________________________
2. ______________________________
3. ______________________________
4. ______________________________
5. ______________________________
6. ______________________________
7. ______________________________
8. ______________________________
9. ______________________________
10. ______________________________
11. ______________________________
12. ______________________________

Answer Key

1. Anxiety disorders
2. Depression
3. Cognitive behavioral therapy
4. Selective serotonin reuptake inhibitors (SSRIs)
5. Bipolar disorder; mood stabilizers
6. Attention deficit/hyperactivity disorder (ADHD); stimulants
7. Obsessive compulsive disorder (OCD)
8. Tourette syndrome
9. Body dysmorphic disorder
10. Eating disorders
11. Down syndrome
12. Autism spectrum disorder

About the Authors

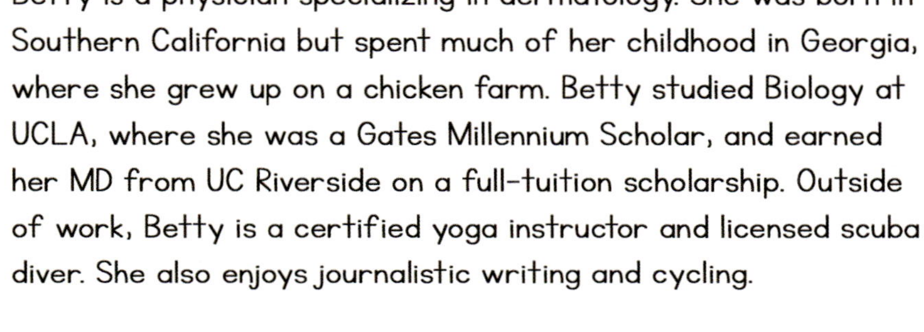

Betty is a physician specializing in dermatology. She was born in Southern California but spent much of her childhood in Georgia, where she grew up on a chicken farm. Betty studied Biology at UCLA, where she was a Gates Millennium Scholar, and earned her MD from UC Riverside on a full-tuition scholarship. Outside of work, Betty is a certified yoga instructor and licensed scuba diver. She also enjoys journalistic writing and cycling.

Dr. Betty Nguyen

Brandon is a physician specializing in ophthalmology. He was born and raised in Southern California. Brandon studied Microbiology, Immunology, and Molecular Genetics at UCLA, where he was a Barry Goldwater Scholar, and earned his MD from Stanford. He is passionate about medical education for students of all ages. In his free time, Brandon enjoys traveling, playing tennis, and performing card magic tricks.

Dr. Brandon Pham

Jake is a physician specializing in psychiatry. He was born in Philadelphia, Pennsylvania but spent most of his childhood in Kennesaw, Georgia. He studied Biological Sciences at the University of Georgia, where he also earned his MBA. He then earned his MD from Thomas Jefferson University in Philadelphia, Pennsylvania. He is passionate about creating educational videos on social media that improve mental health literacy. Jake enjoys traveling, gardening, and playing soccer.

Dr. Jake Goodman

Check out the rest of the books in our series!

Website: mdforkids.org

Instagram: @md.for.kids